KARATE KATA
HEIAN 4

Text and Instructions by
M. NAKAYAMA

Demonstrated by
TERUYUKI OKAZAKI

Published by
KODANSHA INTERNATIONAL LTD.
Tokyo, Japan & Palo Alto, Calif., U.S.A.

*Distributed in the British Commonwealth (excluding Canada)
by Ward Lock & Company Limited., London and Sydney; in
Continental Europe by Boxerbooks, Inc., Zurich; and in the Far
East by Japan Publications Trading Co., C.P.O. Box 722, Tokyo.*

*Published by Kodansha International Ltd., 2–12–21, Otowa,
Bunkyo-ku, Tokyo 112, Japan and Kodansha International/USA,
Ltd., 577 College Avenue, Palo Alto, California 94306.*

*Library of Congress Catalog Card No. 68–26559.
First edition, 1968.*

Contents

DEDICATED
to my teacher
GICHIN FUNAKOSHI

Introduction

Karate is not, and never was, a technique of aggression.

Ever since ways and means of fighting with bare hands and feet were developed and formalized into the art of karate it has been taught and learned as a method of self-defense; and not until a *karateka* ("user of karate") is provoked does he rely on his art to repulse his opponent. The defensive basis of the art is indicated by the fact that all *kata* ("formal exercises") begin with *uke* ("blocking").

Karate is more than a fighting skill—it is a mental discipline from which students learn the value of kindness and sincerity to others. To become an expert the student must develop self-control as well as mastery of the various techniques of the art.

1. What are Kata?

Kata are the formal exercises of karate. They are sequence movements which are learned by the *karateka* in order to develop rhythm and coordination of technique. As such they are an integral part of his training and they are practiced regularly, along with new techniques, strengthening exercises and sparring.

Kata consist of a logical combination of four fundamental movements: *uke* ("blocking"), *tsuki* ("punching"), *uchi* ("striking") and *keri* ("kicking"). As he goes through these movements in the *dōjō* ("practice gym") the *karateka* assumes himself to be surrounded by a number of imaginary enemies. Each movement of his body, hands and feet has its own meaning and function. None is superfluous. They have been developed by past masters of karate through years of practice.

Today there are approximately fifty forms of kata—some date back to the time when karate was first used or were introduced from China during the middle ages, while others were developed fairly recently. Some are simple while others are complicated, some long and some short. But each kata has its own characteristics.

Kata can be roughly divided into two types. There are kata which aim at body-building, muscle-strengthening and hardening the bones—movements in these kata are expansive and give the impression of power and strength. And there are speed training kata, which are designed to produce lightning-fast reflexes.

Because they involve the use of the whole body kata movements are an ideal form of physical exercise. They can be learned and practiced individually or in groups by anyone—young, old, male or female. They can be done for five minutes or an hour at a time, in the *dōjō* or in the privacy of one's own home.

2. Mental Attitude for the Performance of Kata

(1) Ceremonial Bow: Karate training begins and ends with a ceremonial bow. To perform this movement a *musubi-dachi* ("informal stance") is taken with hands relaxed, lightly touching the thighs. The body is then bent forward, while the eyes remain focused straight ahead. Out of respect to his training partner the *karateka* must perform the bow with sincerity.

Courtesy and decorum are the first requirements of the *karateka*. As the famous instructor Funakoshi Gichin often told his pupils: "The spirit of karate is lost without courtesy." And the *karateka* must be courteous, not only in training but also in daily life. Furthermore he must be humble and gentle. Yet the *karateka* must never be servile—he must always perform the kata boldly and with confidence. This combination of boldness and gentleness, which might seem paradoxical to the beginner, ultimately leads to harmony.

(2) Kamae ("posture") and Zanshin ("perfect finish"): After bowing at the center of the *embusen* ("kata performance line") the *karateka* stands with his feet apart, toes pointing outward, in the *hachiji-dachi* ("open-leg stance") before beginning the kata. If the *heisoku-dachi* ("closed-feet stance") is taken the toes are placed together. The *karateka* must avoid being too tense and must not be over-conscious of the movements he is about to make. He must ease the tension in his body, particularly from the joints of the shoulders and the knees, in order to be fully prepared for any slight or sudden movement. Power and concentration should be centered on the *tanden* ("area of the navel"), breathing should be relaxed and the *karateka* must instill in himself a fighting spirit.

The finish of the kata is most important; for no matter how brilliantly the exercises are executed, if the ending is not good the kata is not perfect. And even after the kata is over the *karateka* must not relax. He must return to his original posture and be prepared for further movements. The *zanshin* in Japanese martial arts has always been highly respected and the karate student should remember that it is important not only in training but also in daily life.

3. Performing Kata

(1) Execute kata correctly and in the right order. The number of movements in each kata is fixed and the student must perform them all, in the right order, without making any mistake.

(2) Move accurately on the *embusen* ("performance line"). The *embusen* is the line from which all the kata movements (forward, backward, right and left) are made. The karate student must complete the kata at the spot from which the first movement was made. This is impossible if the wrong steps are taken or the breadth of steps is inconsistent. Intensive training is necessary to perfect this.

(3) Understand the meanings of the various moves and express them fully. The movements of each kata have their own meanings —either offensive or defensive—which the student must understand clearly and express fully.

(4) Be aware of the target. The *karateka* must realize from where his imaginary opponent is attacking, be sure of his target and know when to strike. His attention must not stray from his target, but at the same time he must be aware of further opponents. (Illustrations of how each of the techniques in kata Heian 4 can be applied are shown throughout the book· the *karateka* must always be aware of the purpose of each move as he performs the kata.)

(5) Execute each kata clearly. Not only should the meaning of each move in the kata be clearly understood, but its characteristics should be clearly performed. Each kata should be interpreted according to its own characteristics—always boldly and powerfully, sometimes swiftly, sometimes slowly.

(6) Perform the kata rhythmically. All the moves in a kata are integrally related to each other. They should be performed rhythmically —not jerkily—from start to finish. The end of one kata is directly related to the start of the next.

(7) Remember the three basic rules of rhythm. In the martial arts, as with athletics and other sports, beauty and rhythm are inter-dependent. And the beauty and rhythm of kata are dependent on three factors: "application of power at the right moment," "fluency of movement," and "body flexibility."

A slow kata performed too quickly is spoiled, as is a fast kata performed too slowly. The body must be flexible, always in the right position and never overstrained.

4. Kata Heian 4

Kata Heian 4 is a basic kata which a karate student learns early in his training. Practice can begin as soon as the elementary techniques which are incorporated in the kata have been learned. Mastery of the kata is a requirement of the 5th *kyū* examination.

(1) Footwork: Though Heian 4 is one of the most elementary kata it sometimes presents difficulties, even to advanced *karateka*. This is because many students execute the footwork wrongly, thus failing to end the kata on the *embusen*. Research into the origins of the kata has shown where these common errors lie. If the correct form, which is detailed in the footwork diagram (pp. 12, 13) and in the diagrams throughout the text, is followed the *karateka* will—with practice—be able to end the kata in the position from which the kata was started.

(2) Stances and techniques: The term stance describes the position of the body at various points in the kata and indicates shifts in the center-of-gravity of the performer and changes in the position of his feet. Techniques are defensive or attacking actions which make up the kata, performed by the *karateka* in relation to an imaginary opponent. The force of the whole body is put into each technique and the muscles tense at the imaginary point of contact.

(3) Timing: If the kata has been properly learned, the count—which is given by the instructor, if there is one present—is the same as the number of stances in the kata. However, the instructor will give more counts for beginners since the kata must be clearly broken down into individual movements. There are pauses of about one second at certain points in the kata (see stances 3,4,6, 8,10,15,16,19) while other stances are held just long enough for the corresponding technique to be properly completed. Kata Heian 4 should take about 45 seconds to perform from beginning to end. (Note carefully that there is no separate count for the

right knee blow, Technique 25, as this action is immediately followed by a left knife-hand block, Technique 26.)

(4) Breathing: The breath is exhaled as the performer comes into position on each stance; it is inhaled as he begins the next movement. As in most kata, there are two points near the middle of the kata where the performer utters a shout (called *ki-ai*). The sound must feel as if it comes from the bottom of the stomach and is made by expelling the breath very sharply at the point of tension, thus giving the muscles extra power.

5. Do's and Don t's for Kata Training

  (1) Never rush through the movements.
  (2) Keep calm.
  (3) The benefit of daily training accumulates; so practice each day—even if only for a few minutes.
  (4) Concentrate on the kata you find most difficult.
  (5) Be conscious of the relationship between kata practice and *kumite* (sparring).

6. The Use of this Book

The sequence movements can be followed by reference to the pull-out section at the back of the book and the diagrams on pp. 12, 13. The main text shows details of the stances and techniques —with more thorough treatment of those which cause difficulties or in which mistakes are commonly made (see Technique 13). The application, or meaning, of each technique is illustrated in each instance.

   The name and number of technique comes at the end of each technique, at the position in which the *karateka* finds himself when the technique is completed.

Footwork Diagram

This diagram illustrates the position of the feet at each stage through-out kata Heian 4. The numerals correspond to the stance numbers in the text, and the small circles represent striking points.

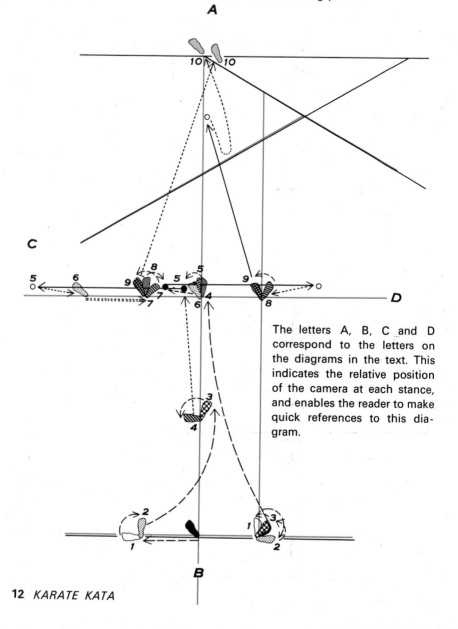

The letters A, B, C and D correspond to the letters on the diagrams in the text. This indicates the relative position of the camera at each stance, and enables the reader to make quick references to this diagram.

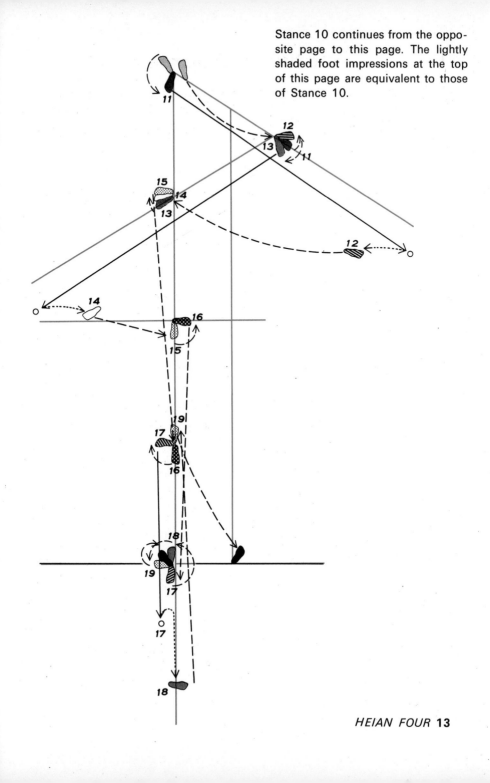

Stance 10 continues from the opposite page to this page. The lightly shaded foot impressions at the top of this page are equivalent to those of Stance 10.

NOTE

Stance numbers are in black.
Technique numbers are in orange.

Kata Heian 4

NATURAL POSITION

This picture is taken with the camera in position A as indicated in the diagram. In some of the following pictures the camera angle changes, so close attention must be given to the corresponding diagram.

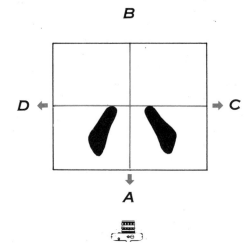

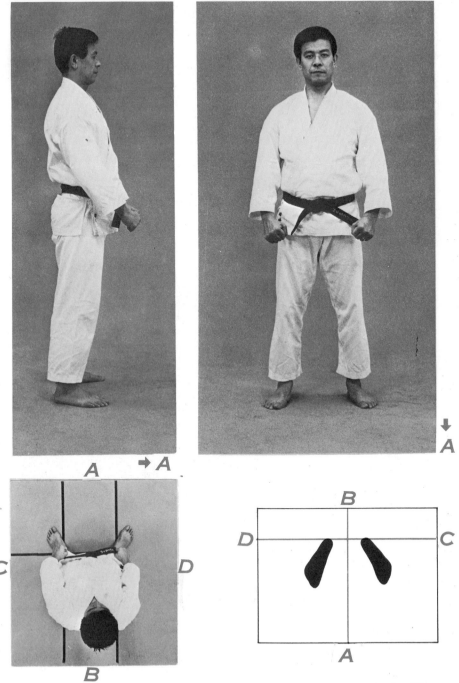

A →A

↓A

C — — D

A — — A

B

B

D — — C

A

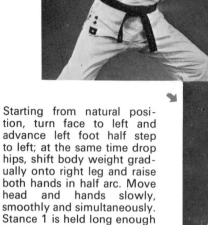

Starting from natural position, turn face to left and advance left foot half step to left; at the same time drop hips, shift body weight gradually onto right leg and raise both hands in half arc. Move head and hands slowly, smoothly and simultaneously. Stance 1 is held long enough to complete the technique.

1 *Migi kōkutsu-dachi*
Right back stance

1 *Hidari-te haiwan hidari sokumen jōdan yoko-uke*
Left back forearm face block with hand open
Migi-te zenwan hitaimae yoko-gamae
Right hand in guard position in front of forehead

Side and top view of Stance 1, Technique 1.

A

C

D

B

→A

APPLICATION: Block attack to face from right side with back of left forearm; then strike with right knife-hand.

Move head and hands slowly, smoothly
and simultaneously.

2 *Hidari kōkutsu-dachi*
Left back stance

2 *Migi haiwan migi sokumen 'jōdan-uke'*
Right back forearm face block with hand open
Hidari zenwan hitaimae 'yoko-gamae'
Left forearm in guard position in front of forehead

D

C

Side and top view of Stance 2, Technique 2.

A

C   D

B

↓
D

APPLICATION: Block attack to face from right side with back of right forearm. Then grab opponent's wrist, draw him close and strike his body with left fist.

DIFFERENT *

A

Slide left foot toward A and at the same time clench and cross fists with right fist on top; thrust downward from right shoulder (see next page).

3 *Hidari zenkutsu-dachi*
Left forward stance

3 *Ryōken gedan 'jūji-uke'*
Two fist downward X-block

A

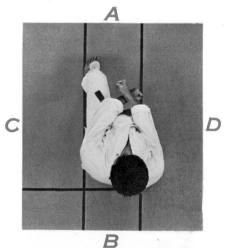

Side and top view of Stance 3, Technique 3.

A

C   D

B

→ A

APPLICATION:
Counter adversary's kick by blocking or striking his shin with two fists.

A

Slide right foot toward left foot while turning hips, before stepping outward toward A (details next page).

Hidari kōkutsu-dachi
Left back stance

Migiken chudan 'morote-uke'
Right augmented forearm block

A

C D

B

→ A

APPLICATION: Block adversary's straight punch; and either counter with left punch, or grab adversary's wrist with left hand and attack with right fist to body.

32 *KARATE KATA*

Turn face to left; rotate hips to right and place both fists at right side of waist (details next page).

Take posture swiftly and smoothly.

5 Migi ashi-dachi
Right foot stance

5 Ryoken 'migi-koshi' kamae
Two fist right side guard position

C

A

Side and top view of Stance 5, Technique 5.

A

C   D

B

➡ A

6 *Hidari uraken jōdan 'yokomawashi-uchi'*
Left sideward back fist strike

Hidari sokutō 'yoko-keage'
Left side snap kick

Techniques 5 and 6 should be executed swiftly with no pause between them.

D ←

→ C

A

→ A

Side and top view of
Technique 6.

A

C

D

B

APPLICATION: As adversary attacks from side retaliate simultaneously with fist and leg to his face, chest, side of stomach or loins. See p. 42 for alternative application (in reverse).

Draw back fist and leg swiftly; rotate hips to left. Then (see next page) thrust right elbow in front of chest to strike left hand which is pulled back.

6 *Hidari zenkutsu-dachi*
Left forward stance

7 *Migi 'enpi-uchi'*
Right elbow strike

No pause between Techniques 6 and 7. There is a slight pause on Stance 6.

D ⟶ A ⟵ C

Side and top view of Stance 6, Technique 7.

APPLICATION: Grab adversary's hand and bring him close in for right elbow attack.

Turn face right; pull back left foot one half-step to right (see next page).

Body faces front but face is turned to right. Bring right leg to inside of left shin and raise right knee; at the same time, place both fists at side of left hip. Without taking this posture correctly it is not possible to make an accurate back fist blow or side kick.

7
Hidari ashi-dachi
Left foot stance

8
Ryōken hidari 'koshi-kamae'
Two fist left side guard position

No pause on this stance before execution of Technique 9.

D   C

A

Side and top view of Stance 7, Technique 8.

A

C

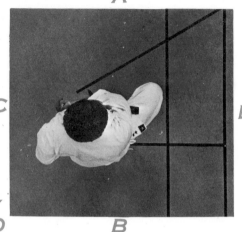

D

D

B

9 *Migi uraken jodan 'yokomawashi-uchi'*
Right sideward back fist strike

Migi sokutō yoko-keage
Right side snap kick

D ← ○ ←————————————● C

Side and top view of Technique 9.

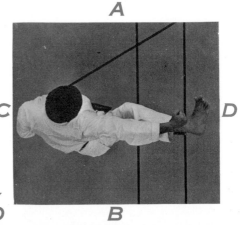

A

C   D

↓
D   B

APPLICATION: Block opponent's punch with back fist and at the same time attack with right side thrust kick. Page 38 shows an alternative application though in reverse.

48 *KARATE KATA*

8
Migi zenkutsu-dachi
Right forward stance

10
Hidari 'enpi-uchi'
Left elbow strike

Techniques 8, 9 and 10 are executed fast with no pause between. There is a slight pause on Stance 8.

D ←

Side and top view of
Stance 8, Technique
10.

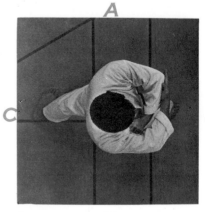

APPLICATION: Strike to
chest of adversary. An elbow
blow will not be effective if
the upper body is bent forward or the shoulder is turned.
It is important to hold hips
firmly in and rotate them with
the strike.

Bring right hand upward to front of face, lower left hand to front of groin; position of feet remains unchanged. Turn hips to left (as shown on next page) and strike out with right hand from front of face to right in a wide half arc in the direction of A; move left hand from below to front of forehead. Hands move continuously and in a circular motion.

9 *Hidari hiza mageru*
Stance with left knee slightly bent

11 *Migi shutō jōdan 'yokomawashi-uchi'*
Right knife-hand strike to neck

Hidarite 'jodan uke'
Left open hand upper block

Stance held long enough to complete the technique.

D

C

A

Side and top view of Stance 9, Technique 11.

A

C   D

B

APPLICATION: Adversary has kicked from the left. Block ankle with edge of left hand; with the same hand—and in one continuous movement—thrust off adversary's arm as he strikes to face; simultaneously, attack opponent's neck with right knife-hand.

12 *Migi jōdan 'mae-keage'*
Right front snap kick

A

Side and top view of
Technique 12.

A

C   D

B

→ A

APPLICATION: This kick is usually
directed at the adversary's Adam's apple,
chin or midriff. But there are cases
(picture right) in which the arm of the
adversary is kicked to break the joint.

Withdraw kicking leg, pull right hand toward chest
and prepare to jump forward toward A.

Withdraw right hand to chest level while clenching fist; bring fist up and in front of chest in a circular motion then down into a back fist strike; simultaneously, extend left hand forward and withdraw to side of left hip as fist is clenched; at the same time jump forward, landing on right foot; and slide left foot behind right heel for support as backward strike is delivered. Fix position of legs and hands simultaneously.

Side view of Technique 13.

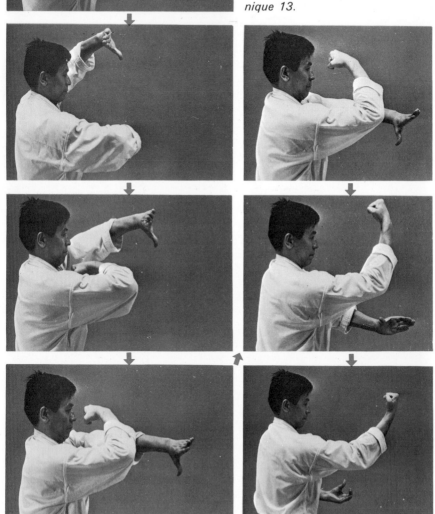

10 *Migi ashi-dachi* Right foot stance

13 *Migi uraken 'tatemawashi-uchi'* Right downward back-fist strike

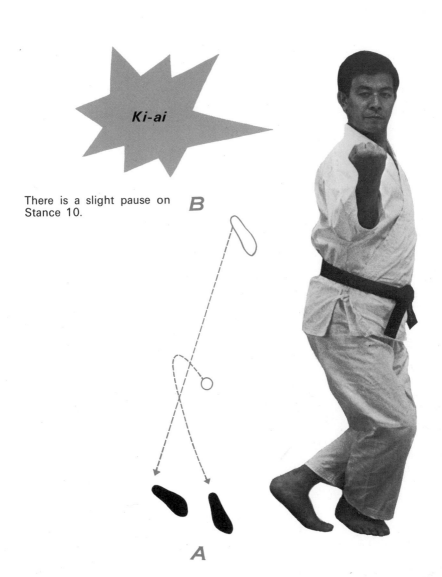

Ki-ai

There is a slight pause on Stance 10.

B

A

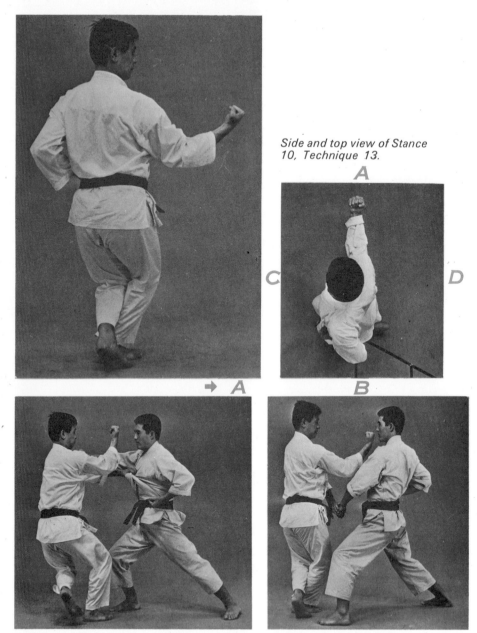

Side and top view of Stance 10, Technique 13.

A

C   D

→ A   B

APPLICATION: (Picture left): Grab opponent by the lapels and bring him close; then attack with downward backfist strike to chest. (Picture right): Block adversary's blow to chest with left hand and attack opponent's face with downward backfist strike.

C

B · A

D

Turn face to left and at the same time rotate hips to left with right leg as pivot; move left foot slantwise to left; cross right fist over left in front of face; bring down both fists (see following page). Note new position of camera.

11 Migi kōkutsu-dachi
Right back stance

14 Ryōken chūdan 'kakiwake-uke'
Closed fist reverse wedge block

This technique should be performed slowly, as if wringing a towel. The stance should be held long enough for the technique to be completed. Then the body tension is relaxed and the front kick (Technique 15) executed.

Side and top view of Stance 11, Technique 14.

A

APPLICATION: This wedge block is used when opponent strikes with both fists (picture left) or when he grabs lapels with both hands. The forearms are brought downward and outward, forcing the adversary's arms apart.

15 *Migi 'mae-keage'*
Right front snap kick

C

B

A

D

While gradually shifting body weight to left leg, execute the kick; do not straighten left knee or change height of hips.

Side and top view of Technique 15.

A

C **D**

B

↓
A

APPLICATION: Following Technique 14, kick to adversary's stomach with right leg without raising hips.

After right front snap
kick, withdraw foot to
above knee level and
thrust forward onto the
floor.

DETAILS OF TECHNIQUE: A right lunge punch is executed at the same time as the right foot is thrust forward to the floor; while making this movement do not pull the right fist back to the right hip but straighten the elbow from the position of the block and thrust the fist forward in a cork-screw punch (Technique 16).

12 *Migi zenkutsu-dachi*
Right forward stance

16 *Migi chūdan 'oi-zuki'*
Right lunge punch to body

There is no pause between this punch (Technique 16) and the left reverse punch (Technique 17).

B

A

D

Side and top view of Stance 12, Technique 16.

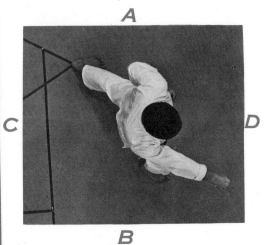

A

C   D

B

↓
A

APPLICATION: Punch to adversary's body.

17

Hidari chūdan 'gyaku-zuki'
Right reverse punch to body

B

A

D

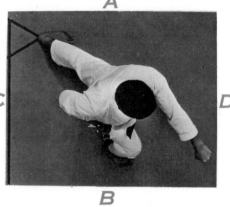

Side and top view of Technique 17.

A

C   D

B

↓
A

APPLICATION: Attack to adversary's midriff; do not elevate hips when delivering consecutive punches.

Turn face to right and at the same time rotate hips to right with weight on left leg which is used as a pivot; change direction by moving right leg to right slantwise; cross both fists in front of face with right fist above; then bring fist down (see next page for details). Level of hips remains constant.

13 *Hidari kōkutsu-dachi*
Left back stance

18 *Ryōken chūdan 'kakiwake-uke'*
Two fist reverse wedge block with fists in front of chest

Stance is held long enough for the technique to be completed.

Side and top view of Stance 13, Technique 18.

A

C

D

↓
A

B

Side and top view of Technique 19.

19 Hidari 'mae-keage'
Left front snap kick

From Stance 13 the left leg is kicked up between fists which remain in the same position.

C

B

A

D

As the left leg is with-
drawn a left lunge
punch is made from the
position of the reverse
wedge block; the blow
strikes the opponent as
soon as the kicking
leg is down (next page).

14 *Hidari zenkutsu-dachi*
Left forward stance

20 *Hidari chudan 'oi-zuki'*
Left lunge punch to body

There is no pause on this stance before the execution of the right reverse punch (Technique 21).

C

B

A

D

Side and top view of Stance 14, Technique 20.

A

C

D

B

Side and top view of Technique 21.

Migi chūdan 'gyaku-zuki'
Right reverse punch to body

After completing lunge punch, attack immediately with reverse punch.

Turn face to left; bend right knee; shift body weight to right leg and move left leg one half step to left; extend fists in augmented left forearm block.

22 *Hidari chūdan 'morote-uke'*
Augmented left forearm block

There is a slight pause
on Stance 15.

C

B

A

Shift body weight to left leg; bend left knee;
and slide right foot one step forward.

16 *Hidari kōkutsu-dachi*
Left back stance

23 *Migi chudan 'morote-uke'*
Right augmented forearm block

There is a slight pause on
Stance 16.

B   A

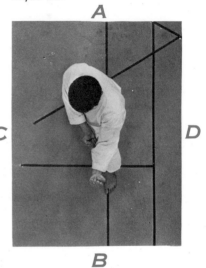

Side and top view of Stance 15, Technique 22.

A

C   D

A

B

Side and top view of Stance 16, Technique 23.

17 *Migi kokutsu-dachi*
Right back stance

24 *Hidari chūdan 'morote-uke'*
Left augmented forearm block

Left foot is brought forward and right foot pivoted through 90 degrees; left arm is extended supported by right fist at elbow. There is no pause between Techniques 22, 23 and 24 which are all executed swiftly.

B

A

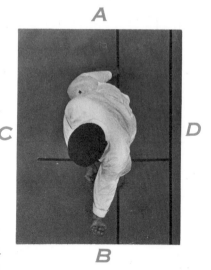

Side and top view of Stance 17, Technique 24.

A

C   D

B

⬇
A

APPLICATION: Inside block to outside of opponent's arm (left) and inside block to inside of opponent's arm.

Position of feet remain
same, left knee is bent.

Turn hips to left and push forward; bend and shift body weight to left knee;
open both hands and thrust forward to head level, palms facing about ten
inches apart.

A

C   D

*Top view of position
between Technique
24 and 25.*

B

APPLICATION: If an adversary strikes with fists or tries to grab the lapels, thrust out both hands, bring elbows inside his arms and grab his head (see next page).

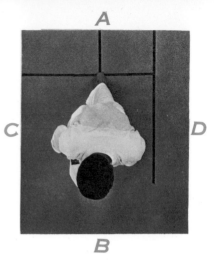

Side and top view of
Technique 25.

APPLICATION: After adversary's head has been grabbed, pull down and hit face sharply with right knee. This is a most effective defense technique.

25 *Migi 'hiza-uchi'*
Right knee blow

Ki-ai

Strike high with right knee and at the same time clench both fists and bring them down strongly on both sides of knee. The body is tense to give maximum power yet it is moving forward, so there is no pause at this point.

B O ←———————— A

Bring right leg in the direction of B; simultaneously rotate hips to the left and turn around; move right hand up to front of midriff; bring left hand up to right ear and strike down in slanting blow with knife-hand.

Turning point for next movement

18 *Migi kōkutsu-dachi*
Right back stance

26 *Hidari 'shutō-uke'*
Left knife-hand block

There is a slight pause on this stance.

B   A

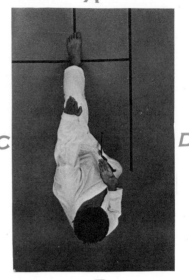

Side and top view of Stance 18, Technique 26.

A

C   D

B

↓

A APPLICATION: Block with left knife-hand and attack adversary's neck with right knife-hand.

Without shifting the level of hips thrust them forward and rotate them to left; at the same time slide right foot forward and move right hand upward and then down from left ear in knife-hand.

Side and top view of Stance 19, Technique 27.

A

C   D

B

↓
A

APPLICATION: Block with right knife-hand, grab and twist adversary's wrist and attack with left fist or spear-hand.

19
Hidari kōkutsu-dachi
Left back stance

27
Migi 'shutō-uke'
Right knife-hand block

B

A

There is a definite pause on this stance.

NATURAL POSITION

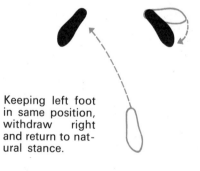

Keeping left foot in same position, withdraw right and return to natural stance.

Glossary of Japanese Karate Terms

The pronunciation of Japanese words is very simple: the vowels are like those in Italian and the consonants like those in English (g is always hard). There are no silent letters (e.g., mae-keage =ma-e-ke-a-ge).

Ashi: Leg or foot.

Chūdan: Middle.

Dachi: Stance.
Dan: Grade.
Dōjō: Gymnasium or practice hall.

Embusen: Kata performance line.
Enpi: Elbow.
Enpi-uchi: Elbow strike.

Gedan: Lower area of the body.
Gyaku-zuki: Reverse punch.

Hachiji-dachi: Open-leg stance.
Haiwan: Back-arm.
Heisoku-dachi: Closed-feet stance.
Hidari: Left.
Hidari-te: Left-hand.
Hitai-mae: In front of forehead.
Hiza: Knee.
Hiza-uchi: Knee strike.

Jōdan: Face area.
Jūji-uke: X-block.

Kakiwake-uke: Reverse wedge-block.
Kamae: Posture.
Karateka: User of karate.
Keage: Snap kick.
Ken: Fist.
Keri: Kicking.
Ki-ai: Loud, deep cry from bottom of stomach.
Kōkutsu-dachi: Back stance.
Koshi: Hips.
Kyū: Class.

Mae-keage: Front snap kick.
Mageru: Bend.
Migi: Right.
Migi-te: Right hand.
Morote: Both hands.
Musubi-dachi: Informal stance, feet turned out.

Oi-zuki: Lunge punch.

Ryōken: Two fists.

Shizen tai: Natural posture.
Shutō: Knife-hand.
Sokutō: Foot-edge.

Tanden: Area of the navel.
Tate-mawashi-uchi: Downward curving strike.
Tsuki: Punch.

Uchi: Striking.
Uke: Blocking.
Uraken: Back fist.

Yoko: Side.
Yoko-kamae: Side stance.

Yoko-keage: Side snap kick.
Yoko-mawashi-uchi: Side roundhouse blow.
Yoko-uke: Side block.

Zanshin: Completion of the technique in which awareness of opponent and surroundings are maintained.
Zenkutsu dachi: Forward stance.
Zenwan: Forearm.
Zuki: Punch.